Hojoki

THE ROCK SPRING COLLECTION
OF JAPANESE LITERATURE

HOJOKI

Visions of a Torn World

Text by Kamo-no-Chomei

translated by
Yasuhiko Moriguchi and David Jenkins

with illustrations by
Michael Hofmann

Stone Bridge Press • *Berkeley, California*

Published by

Stone Bridge Press, P.O. Box 8208, Berkeley, CA 94707

TEL 510-524-8732 • sbp@netcom.com • www.stonebridge.com

The quotation on page 11 is from "Andrei Rublëv" by Andrei
Tarkovsky, translated by Kitty Hunter Blair (London: Faber and
Faber, 1991).

Cover design by David Bullen
incorporating a painting by Michael Hofmann

Text design by Peter Goodman

Printed in the United States of America

10 9 8 7 6 5 4 3 2 1

ISBN 1-880656-22-1

*F*or the people of South Hyogo

Contents

❀ ❀ ❀

He hears snatches of conversation; the wind singing under the thatched eaves; the rustle of twigs . . . the full-throated, happy cry of swallows in the evening air. His eyes are filled with helpless anguish, like someone who has suddenly lost the power of speech at the very moment when he is about to say something terribly important, something crucial to everyone who might hear it.

FROM THE SCREENPLAY
"ANDREI RUBLËV" BY ANDREI TARKOVSKY,
TRANSLATED BY KITTY HUNTER BLAIR

Introduction

Yuku kawa no nagare wa taezushite

shikamo moto no mizu ni arazu

yodomi ni ukabu utakata wa

katsu kie katsu musubite

hisashiku todomaritaru tameshi nashi

yononaka ni aru hito to sumika to

mata kaku no gotoshi

*T*his is the prelude to *Hojoki*, the great work of literary witness of medieval Japan by the recluse Kamo-no-Chomei (1155–1216). These lines are, together with the portentous tolling of the Gion bell at the start of the contemporaneous *Heike Monogatari*, the most familiar opening lines in Japanese literature. Supple and melodious, they prefigure the language and substance of the entire piece that follows.

Hojoki was composed in 1212, when its author was in his late fifties. A mix of social chronicle and personal testimony, it is a comparatively short work organized in three main parts. The first tells of a series of calamities, personally observed by Chomei, that overtook Kyoto in the late Heian Period. The last part is a record of Chomei's thoughts and life in retirement from the world in the mountains southeast of the capital, a life brought about in part by disinheritance from a prominent ecclesiastical family, in part by a desire to find meaning and peace in a nonmaterialistic world. The two parts pivot on a central section that is a scathing commentary on the human condition.

Basil Bunting, who based his poetic "condensation," *Chomei at Toyama*, on an Italian prose translation of the work, wrote: "The *Ho-Jo-Ki* is in prose, but the careful proportion and balance of the parts, the leitmotif of the House running through it, and some other indications, suggest that he intended a poem, more or less elegiac; but had not time, nor possibly energy, at his then age, to work out what would have been for Japan an entirely new form, nor to condense his material sufficiently. This I have attempted to do for him."

However, there is nothing provisional about *Hojoki*, and nothing tentative, beyond Chomei's exhausted probing of the integrity of his purpose, indeed his questioning of his own sanity, toward the close of the piece. These very elements give the work an intense humanity from which it ultimately derives its timelessness.

There can be no question as to the essentially poetic intent of *Hojoki*. From the first lines, we are clearly aware of an enhancement of language that carries its subject in a crafted, rhythmic manner. Even someone ignorant of the Japanese language can detect in the romanized transliteration a restless rippling, and hear the stuttering gush of water over the consonants. There are countless other examples, for instance in the quickening of pace in the description of the fire. Words fly through the air like the cinders the writer is describing, in a flurry of staccato, "journalistic" in its best sense. This man was *there*, and eight centuries later, he is still out of breath. Again, later, in one of the most beautiful passages of the whole work he describes his companionship with a little boy, son of the warden of his mountain retreat; the language rises in visionary warmth as he describes solitary nights by his fireside, recalling his friends, hearing in the song of the copper pheasants the voices of his parents.

This musical "charge"—what Pound termed *melopoeia*—is coupled with a compelling visual dimension (*phanopoeia*). Again, from the opening lines we gain a clear pictorial image of the rushing water, the gathering and dispersing of the froth on its surface, but also of a setting of hillside rocks through which this river flows. Elsewhere, we see the fire engulfing Kyoto, spreading "like an unfolding fan," just as later we share the visions of the fishermen's braziers in a little cooking fire.

Then beyond this, most subtly, we encounter *logopoeia*, Pound's "dance of the intellect among words," in which words are employed not only for their plain meaning but for their cargo of nuance, irony, or association. Thus, in the opening lines, a man's home is *sumika*, carrying the resonance of "abode," "dwelling," even approaching its modern biological sense of "habitat." Or when describing the city of Kyoto as *tamashiki-no-miyako*, we are not to understand this as a capital glittering like a veritable jewel but more as a kind of gilded lily, "glorious" in the direction of "vainglorious."

In structure too, as Bunting noted, the intention

is poetic. The three sections—the disasters, the central pivot, and the latter hermitage—are held together by the recurring image of the House. First, we see the lofty towers—perhaps indeed jewel-encrusted—of the well-to-do. These appear almost to have a life of their own as they assert their dominance over the rooftops of lesser citizenry. But all the houses, together with their inhabitants, are buffeted and destroyed with supreme indifference by nature and by man alike. A fire that starts in an entertainers' lodging house levels a major section of the city, reducing to ash both imperial chambers and common dwellings. A whirlwind destroys fences, so that you are no longer able to differentiate between your property and that of your neighbor. A capricious imperial decree orders the removal of the capital, so the ambitious office seeker must dismantle his house, float it down the river to the new location, re-erect it, and then, upon a new decree, pull it down again. Famine and disease reduce the most distinguished households, and even chopping up your home for firewood will provide heat for no more than a day. And of course an earthquake simply brings the whole thing down around your ears. The Imperial Household is transferred to present-day Kobe, where the new "palace" has the aspect of a log cabin, comically conceded by Chomei to be not without a certain antique charm. Through the latter part of the book, Chomei's own social decline is conveyed in the progressively smaller houses he builds, deeper and deeper in the mountains. He finally builds a tiny hut, which gives *Hojoki* its name—literally "Writings from a Place Ten Feet Square"—and which in a memorable image becomes so overgrown we feel it almost melting into the side of the mountain.

This sense of the little dwelling sinking into the earth is part of a further skein of symbolism, formed from the four elements of nature, that also binds the work together. The work starts with the confident rippling of water, and closes with Chomei "well into my sixth decade / when the dew of life disappears." The violent earthquake that topples mountains in the first part of the work is mirrored in a more benevolent earth gently embracing the hermit's last home. The gales and floods that precede the terrible pestilence stand in contrast to "Autumn Breezes" and "Flowing Water," the songs he later plays to himself on koto and biwa. The devastating fire of 1177, with the flames leaping whole blocks, faintly echoes in the companionship he finds in the dying embers of his own little fire in the woods. Then, each element is often interplayed with the other three with considerable deftness. A fearful wind feeds the spreading conflagration, the earthquake forces water to gush from cracked rocks, the capital itself depends upon the earth, the fruits of the surrounding countryside. Later, the snow melts to the earth in a striking image of the redemption of sin.

Clearly, Chomei's intentions go far beyond the desire to make a platitudinous point on the question of the transience of man and his property. There is a sophisticated political attitude here, as well as a conscious crafting of textured image. But his rejection of the world is also a kind of edifice to which he feels dangerously attached, and he tells us as much. While he sets out a forthright statement on the abasements of materialism, we are also made conscious of an agonized ambivalence. We gain a suspicion that his own spiritual "construct" is also perilously close to collapse, and that he closes not in the silence of acceptance and wisdom, but in an anguished, despairing speechlessness.

Chomei was born in 1155, second son of Kamo-no-Nagatsugu, who held the rank of *sho-negi* at the Kamo Shrine, consisting of Kamigamo (upper

Kamo) and Shimogamo (lower Kamo) shrines in northeastern Kyoto. His father's rank was that of a quite senior prelate, master of Shimogamo. The rank also carried court influence and responsibilities. At the age of six, Chomei was accorded an official Court rank, also relatively senior.

From an early age his chief passions were music and poetry, and since succession to a position in one of the Kamo shrines appeared to be preordained, he felt able to indulge them. However, his family relations were complex, and the conduct of both secular and religious affairs of the day plagued by intrigue and corruption. Additionally, the young Chomei, as a precociously successful poet, cannot be said to have been the model of modesty and discretion.

Chomei was a member of important poetry circles, was successful in major poetry competitions, and was published in an imperial anthology (the *Senzaiwakashu*) by the age of thirty-two. What distinguished him from his fellows, however, was a fierce sense of social compassion. This is commonly thought to have developed later as a result of his disinheritance from the family positions and adoption of the Buddhist faith. However, as a young man he clearly went out of his way to witness the "many awful happenings" that befell the citizens of Kyoto and records them with a degree of engagement that would have been unthinkable to his literary contemporaries. The master poet Fujiwara-no-Teika (1162–1241) stated his own social attitude clearly enough: "My ears are filled with news of uprisings and killings. . . . I care nothing about such matters."

The first of these, for Chomei, defining events was the great fire in the spring of 1177, shortly after the death of his father. The whirlwind followed in the spring of 1180. The capital was moved to Settsu (or Tsu) in the summer of that year. The famine occurred over the next two years. The earthquake took place in 1185. Moving busily among the people in such terrible circumstances, Chomei cannot fail to have noticed the growing influence of the populist Buddhist movements led by reformist priests, particularly Honen, who was to die the year Chomei completed *Hojoki*.

However, even as these contemporary events were leaving their mark on his thinking, Chomei was pursuing a career as establishment poet. Eventually, some twenty-five of his poems were published in imperial anthologies, ten of them in the great *Shinkokin-wakashu*, presented to the emperor in 1205.

But Chomei was never one to ingratiate himself politically, nor unduly to endear himself to the powerful and the useful. Pursuit of the arts was surrounded by intricate etiquette, and a sometimes trivial-seeming act could have serious political consequences. For instance, in a famous episode, Chomei and some friends were having a music party and, carried away, Chomei played a biwa piece known as "Takuboku," secretly passed down from teacher to follower and not to be performed unsanctioned in public. This earned him a rebuke from the Cloistered Emperor Gotoba.

In 1201, Chomei was selected as one of the thirteen members of the newly reconstituted Poetry Order (*Waka-dokoro*), mostly consisting of highly ranked nobles. Only Chomei and one other were of lesser rank, and quite possibly not entitled even to sit on the same level of floor as their "peers."

In the course of his life as a poet, Chomei not only contributed to imperial anthologies, but also compiled a volume of his own poetry, *Kamo-no-Chomei-shu* (1181), a collection of about a hundred poems thought to have been written in his twenties. He also compiled a series of essays on poetry, *Mumyo-sho*, probably while working on *Hojoki*, which set out his thoughts on the writing of poems, with criticism and biography, as well as notes on manners appropriate to poetry meetings. Toward the very end of his life appeared *Hosshin-shu*—*hosshin* meaning "to aspire to *satori*"—a collection of exemplary stories about Buddhist monks.

This body of work and the poetry itself reveals Chomei to be an accomplished poet, with a graceful use of imagery and in firm control of language, also with clear concerns as to the intellectual and social context of the work. Yet as a poet he is not generally thought to share the towering distinction of many of his contemporaries, such as Teika, one of the principal compilers of the *Shinkokin-wakashu*, or Teika's father, Fujiwara-no-Shunzei, one of the more celebrated of that collection's poets, or the wayfarer Saigyo. It is *Hojoki* that provides Chomei not only that distinction, but an undisputed place in world literature.

❀ ❀ ❀

*I*n 1204 Chomei became a Buddhist monk and moved to the country at Ohara, near Kyoto. Four years later, he moved to Hino, to the southeast of the city, and that is where he built the last of his huts.

Whatever finally precipitated his act of self-exile, it has been remarked that in leaving the world he discovered his sense of it, in particular a remarkable historical perspective. His own era was one of transition, a time of the final collapse of the power of the Heian court in Kyoto and the emergence of a series of military governments in Kamakura ruled by shogun. The period is considered the end of *kodai* (ancient times) and the beginning of *chusei* (middle ages), a time in which people seeking the protection of the powerful were giving away their property, and more and more of this property was coming into the ownership of noble families and major temples and shrines, as well as the emerging military class. This was a time of fierce political struggle as well as major civil disorder, and eventually civil war.

Such a world, with its dislocations and general sense of discontinuity, one might be happy to leave. But for Chomei's reasons for renouncing the world, we rely on two anecdotes.

The first he recounts himself in his *Mumyo-sho* and it illustrates Chomei's lack of political tact in his family relations, particularly with his powerful relative Kamo-no-Sukekane, who had become *negi*, or chief administrator, of the Kamo shrines. Chomei entered a poem containing the phrase ". . . *ishikawaya-semi-no-ogawa* . . ." in an official poetry competition. The poem was judged to have lost, the phrase being held to refer to a nonexistent river. There was a protest, and it is possible Chomei himself spread a rumor that the judging had been unfair. Judging was then entrusted to another poet. The new judge, also unfamiliar with the phrase, decided to consult Chomei before making a decision. Chomei explained that the phrase was an alternative name for the Kamo River and could easily be found in histories of the shrine. This incident became a famous humiliation for Sukekane (never on the best of terms with Chomei anyway), who was undoubtedly offended because someone in his position was shown to be insufficiently familiar with the history of his own shrine. Making matters worse, Chomei's poem was included in the *Shinkokin-wakashu*.

The second episode appears in the diary of Minamoto-no-Ienaga, an official of the high-ranking Poetry Circle, or *Waka-dokoro*. A position as head of the shrine Tadasu-no-yashiro, part of the Kamo complex, became vacant. This position was customarily a stepping stone to that of *sho-negi* of Shimogamo itself, and in light of Chomei's father's former occupancy of it, Emperor Gotoba considered Chomei the man to fill it. Sukekane vehemently opposed the appointment. He thought that his own eldest son should get the job because, though much younger, his son had the higher rank and had worked for the shrine longer than Chomei. On hearing of Sukekane's objections, Goto-ba felt obliged to withdraw the appointment. Instead he sought to raise the status of another shrine and install Chomei as *negi* there. However, by this time Chomei had lost interest, as well as all ambition. (Later, after Chomei's own death, Sukekane's son was to meet a violent end.)

How thoroughgoing Chomei's retreat from the world was is far from clear. He tells of revisiting the capital unashamed of his appearance as "a begging monk" and seems to have kept himself well informed of happenings in the city, although he severed connections with many of his previous circles. Strangely, in 1211, the year before he completed *Hojoki*, Chomei made the journey to Kamakura in the east, to visit the shogun, Sanetomo, also a poet. The purpose of this journey is unknown, although it has been suggested he wished to exert some kind of literary influence upon Sanetomo. In this he was almost certainly unsuccessful.

❋ ❋ ❋

*A*s in so many other cases before and since, Chomei, in retiring from the world, became the true wanderer in it. He and his work transcend not only place, but time too. Chomei's literary immortality resides in *Hojoki* itself, in his unflinching determination to bear witness to his age, in defiance of the literary conventions of the day. The witness is conveyed in a remarkable range of tones, irascible, scholarly, compassionate, and self-mocking, with occasional pawky certitudes, even belligerence. But there is also an essential self-doubt in which the writer reveals not only his face, but his soul.

The impact of this work—the calamities, the witness, the luster of the commentary, the retirement—would be extraordinary enough, and the riches of the language a full enough reward. However, at the very end of the piece, Chomei creates a moment that is quite startling: he seems to open a door in the text and steps through, to address not us, but himself. He seems almost physically stricken by the realization that his minimal life in his hut has itself become an attachment to the world of illusion. His retreat from the world of sin and self-delusion has perhaps itself been sinful and has led to a stunning perception of emptiness and even insanity. It is at this moment that we see the true saintliness of this great man.

And to those who wish to know how they might bear witness in their own troubling times, Chomei says this:

> *To understand*
> *the world of today,*
> *hold it up*
> *to the world*
> *of long ago.*

Hojoki

An asterisk indicates an annotation in the Notes.

*T*he flowing river
never stops
and yet the water
never stays
the same.

Foam floats
upon the pools,
     scattering, re-forming,
never lingering long.

     So it is with man
and all his dwelling places
here on earth.

❀ ❀ ❀

*I*n our glorious capital
the roof tops of the houses
of the high and lowly
stand in line and seem to
jostle for prominence.

They appear to have endured
for generations, but look more closely—
those that have stood for long
are few indeed.

One year they burn down
and the next are raised again.

Great houses fade away,
to be replaced by lesser ones.

        Thus too those
        who live in them.

The place itself
does not change,
nor do the crowds.
    Even so, of all
    the many people I once knew
    only one or two remain.

    They are born into dusk
    and die as the day dawns,
        like that foam
        upon the water.

People die
and are born—

        whence they come
        and where they go,
        I do not know.

Nor do I understand
the transitory homes they build.

For whom do they fret themselves?
What can be so pleasing to the eye?

A house and its master
are like the dew that gathers
on the morning glory.

Which will be the first to pass?

Sometimes the dew falls away
while the flowers stay.

But they will surely
wilt in the morning sun.

Sometimes the flower shrivels
while the dew holds on.

But it will not
outlive the day.

❀ ❀ ❀

*I*n the forty years or so
since I reached the age
to understand the heart of things,
I have witnessed
many awful happenings.

One night long ago
  —it would be the twenty-eighth day
  of the fourth month
  of the third year of Angen*—
a loud wind was blowing.

At eight o'clock a fire broke out
in the southeast of the city,
then spread north and west.

The fire finally reached
the south gate of the Palace.
This gate, together with the State Chamber,
University hall, and Office of the Interior,
all burned to ashes in one night.

They say it started
at Higuchi-Tominokoji,*
in the lodgings of a company of dancers.

The wind blew wildly—
  this way! that way!—
and the fire spread,
  like an unfolding fan.

Houses far away
engulfed in smoke!

Closer by, hungry flames
licked the ground.

Sky crimson all about!
Cinders flashing,
lit by fire!

Flames driven by
unrelenting gusts
flew whole blocks.

    Who, in all this,
    would not be scared to death?

Some suffocated by smoke
fell upon the ground.
Some swallowed by flames
died at once.

Some scarce able
to save themselves,
lost all their worldly goods.

Many treasures
reduced to ash!

Dreadful,
dreadful loss!

The fire destroyed
sixteen noble houses—
who knows how many more?—
    I heard one third
    of the entire capital.

Scores of men and women perished.

Countless horses,
countless cattle,
    also died.

        All of man's doings are senseless
        but spending his wealth
        and tormenting himself
        to build a house in this hazardous city
        is especially foolish.

*T*hen
    in the fourth month
    of the fourth year of Jisho*
came a great whirlwind,
which struck Nakamikado-Kyogoku*
and blew as far as Rokujo.

It blasted three, four city blocks.

No house, big or small,
once caught by this wind,
was left unscathed.

Some were leveled,
some left with only
posts and beams.

The wind wrenched off gates
and dropped them blocks away.

It flung down fences
so that one plot of land
merged with the next.

Household goods
were tossed into the sky.

Thatch and shingles
danced wildly in the wind,
like winter leaves.

Dust rose like smoke
so nothing could be seen.

The din so intense
no human voice could be heard.

      The very winds of hell
      must be this loud!

Not only houses
were destroyed.

Many people too
were hurt, maimed
trying to save their homes.

Then the wind moved south
and caused more grief.

      Winds often blow—
      but ever with such force?

It was all so freakish
I thought it must
be an omen.

*A*nd then
      in the sixth month
      of that fourth year of Jisho
the capital was suddenly moved.

This was deeply shocking.

I understand the city of Kyoto
was founded in the reign of Saga,*
so by now some four hundred years had passed.

Not an easy matter
to transplant it on a whim.

Small wonder
people muttered,
      angrily.

But protest was to no avail,
and first the emperor,

then ministers,
then nobles of the highest rank,
all moved to the new capital.

Who in high office
could stay behind?

Those who yet craved rank or position
and depended on the patronage of masters
tried to move as quickly as they could.

Those who had missed their chance,
had failed to gain office,
or had otherwise lost hope,
were left behind, lamenting.

Once-proud mansions
fell to ruin as the days went by.

Houses were demolished
and floated down the Yodo River,*
while the ground where they had stood
turned into fields before your eyes.

People's values also changed.
They preferred horse and saddle—
no need now for ox or coach.

All now sought estates
in the south and west.
No one wanted land
in the north and east.

Around that time
some business took me
to this new capital
in the country of Tsu.

When I saw the place
I thought it cramped indeed.
No space for city blocks.

In the north
the land rose
toward the hills.

In the south
it sloped away,
down to the sea.

Everywhere,
the crash of waves,
and strong sea breezes.

The palace in the hills
brought to mind
an ancient wooden lodge,
somehow odd enough
to give an air of elegance.

I wondered where
they were building houses
with the wood from those
dismantled day by day,
bottling up the river,

for there were still many empty lots
and few standing houses.

The old capital was in ruins
while the new was yet to rise.

Everyone felt adrift,
    clouds.

The natives of the place
had lost their land
and were distraught.

Those moving there
sighed at the chore
of having to build anew.

When you looked around
those you might expect in carriages
were now on horseback.

Those you thought
to see in court attire
were in common dress.

The style of the capital
had suddenly changed.
Former gentlemen now seemed
mere provincial soldiers.

    All this was felt to be
    prelude to civil chaos.

Sure enough,
time passed and
    confusion, anguish
    filled the hearts of all.

Indeed, grievances grew so acute
that this same winter
the capital was returned.

But what of houses
now destroyed?
They could not
be built again
exactly as before.

    I have heard
    that in the distant past,
    this nation was governed
    with compassion
    by certain wise rulers.*

    The palace was thatched
    with common reeds,
    the eaves left ragged.

    When the emperor saw
    smoke rise thinly
    from the people's hearths
    he waived already modest taxes.

    This was
    an act of mercy,

a desire to help
his people.

To understand
the world of today,
hold it up
to the world
of long ago.

*L*ater
(was it in the Yowa era?*
—so long ago that I forget)
came a famine lasting two full years
brought much misery.

First, in spring and summer,
there was drought.
Then in autumn,
gales and floods.

These terrible events
came one upon another.

Finally, the grain crops failed.

People plowed in spring
and planted in summer,
but in vain.

There was no happy bustle
of autumn harvest
        of laying away in winter.

In every region
people gave up farms and homes.
Others left for the hills.

Many prayers were chanted,
        rituals performed,
with no result.

Kyoto always has relied
on the countryside
but now supplies stopped
and soon all dignity was lost.

People steeled themselves
to sell off possessions,
        now of no value.

There was a little trade,
but grain was worth
more than gold.

Beggars were many in the streets,
        clamor of suffering,
            sorrow filled the air.

In this way, the year
struggled to its close.

There was hope
things might improve
the following year.

But then on top of all
a great plague broke out,
        stood the world upon its head.

Everyone was starving.
Time passed and things grew worse
—people seemed like fish
in a shrinking pool.

Decorously dressed folk,
in hats and gaiters,
went from house to house,
frantically begging.

Even as you watched,
stricken people walking by
would suddenly fall.

So many bodies of the starved
lay in the streets
hard by the walls of houses.

Since these were not removed
there rose a dreadful stench.
It was more than one could bear
to look upon these rotting corpses!

Worse still beside the river—
    not even room
for horse and cart to pass.

The woodcutters also starving,
    firewood disappeared.

With nothing else
some tore down their homes
and took the wood to market.

It was said the value
of this wood
was not enough to live on
for one day.

Then, I was baffled
finding kindling painted red,
and catching glimpses
of gold leaf.

I inquired and found
someone had been reduced
to breaking into temples,
and stealing images of Buddha,
tearing out the fittings of the halls
and chopping them to bits.

    Sinful times!
    That I should witness
    such a dreadful thing!

But then so many other sights
to break the heart.

Loving couples—
        the one whose love was deeper
        always died first.

They held back,
        gave the meager food
        to their dearest.

In families,
parents always were the first
to pass away.

I saw babies lying,
        still sucking breast,
unaware their mothers were already dead.

A certain monk,
        Ryugyo-hoin
        of Ninnaji,
felt great pity for the
multitudes of dying.

When he came upon a dying man
he performed last rites,
traced the holy mark*
upon the brow.

To keep tally of the dead
he counted two full months.

On the streets of Kyoto
     bounded north and south
     by Ichijo and Kujo,
     east and west
     by Kyogoku and Suzaku*
the corpses numbered
forty thousand.

This did not include
the many, many
dead before or since.

Add to this the outskirts
     by the river, in Shirakawa,*
     Nishi-no-kyo, and other parts
and the provinces
along the seven highways.

         Dead without number.

I hear tell
of another such calamity
in the past,
     in the days of Emperor Sutoku
     in the years of Chosho.*

But I know nothing
of that time.

     All I know is this was
     the very worst
     I have seen.

Soon after
    —I wonder now, when was it?*—
a great quake
shook the earth.

This too was
a terrible event.

Mountains fell
and filled the rivers.

The seas heaved
and flooded the land.

The earth itself split
and water gushed out.

Giant rocks cracked
and rolled down
into the valleys.

Boats along the shore
were helpless in the waves.

Horses on the streets
stumbled as they walked.

Around the capital
not one temple or pagoda
remained intact.

Some collapsed
and some fell over.

Dust and ashes rose
like billows of smoke.

Earth shaking,
houses breaking
sounded like the crash
of falling thunderbolts.

Caught inside
a house might crush you.

Outside, the ground was torn apart.

Without wings
you could not fly away.
Only a dragon
may ride the clouds!

Surely such an earthquake
is the most terrifying of events.

In time the violent shaking stopped,
but aftershocks continued.

Every day twenty, thirty quakes,
each one frightening enough
in normal times.

Only after ten or twenty days
did they begin to ease.

Sometimes there were
four, five shocks
then two or three,
then fewer and fewer.

These aftershocks lasted
for about three months.

Of the four elements,*
water, fire, and wind
often cause great damage.
Earth does not so often
bring catastrophe.

Long before
        in the years of Saiko*
there had been an earthquake.
That one even caused the head
of the Great Buddha at Todaiji to fall,
        as well as many other fearful things.

But from all I hear
that was no equal
to this quake.

For a while right after
there was talk
of the vanities of this world,

and people seemed to be rid
of the sinfulness in their hearts.

But days and months went by,
then years,
and no one spoke of it again.

❀ ❀ ❀

*S*o as we see
our life is hard
in this world.

We and our houses
fleeting, hollow.

Many troubles
flow from your status,
social rank.

The lowly man
who lives beside the man of power
cannot openly rejoice,
even when glad.

And when sorrow
becomes intolerable
he never can cry out.

His anxious air,
his constant fearful trembles,

are those of a sparrow
near the nest of a hawk.

The poor man
who lives near the rich
is shamed by shabbiness.

He goes in and out
by day or night
with self-effacing air.

He sees the envy of
his wife, children, servants.

He knows the rich despise them all
and his heart is troubled.

Never, never
can he find peace.

If you live
among crowds
you cannot flee
when fire breaks out.

If you wish to live
far from others,
traveling is hard
and there is danger of thieves.

The powerful are greedy.
Those who stand alone are always mocked.

Men of means
have much to fear.

Those with none
know only bitterness.

If you entrust yourself
to the care of others
you will be owned by them.

If you care for others
you will be enslaved
by your own solicitude.

If you conform to the world
it will bind you hand and foot.

If you do not, then
it will think you mad.

> And so the question,
> where should we live?
> And how?

> Where to find
> a place to rest a while?

> And how bring
> even short-lived peace
> to our hearts?

❀ ❀ ❀

*A*s for me,
I came into property*
from my father's mother.

I lived there a long while
but then came death,
          my family split*
and I came down in the world.

Memories were warm
but I could not stay and
          after thirty,
by myself, I built a house
one-tenth the size
of my former home.

I built a simple living space,
but had no means to build
what most would think
a proper house.

I put up outer walls
but could not afford a gate.

I set up bamboo poles
as shelter for my cart.

When it snowed
or when the wind blew
my house felt precarious.

It was near the river
so danger from flooding
always loomed.
The place was also
overrun with thieves.

In much this way,
with often troubled mind,
I struggled on for thirty years
in this unkind world.

In this time,
my best intentions foiled,
I came to understand
my hopeless luck.

    Therefore,
in my fiftieth spring
I retired from the world.

In any case, I had no wife or child,
no family to regret.

I had no rank,
no revenues,
so where the worldly ties?

In idleness
I lay down on Mount Ohara,*
    clouds my pillow,
and some five springs
and autumns went by.

Then,
well into my sixth decade,
when the dew of life disappears,
I built a little hut,
a leaf from which
the last drops might fall.

I was a wayfarer
raising a rude shelter,
an old silk worm
spinning one last cocoon.

Unlike the house of my middle years,
this not even one hundredth the size.

The fact is
I get older,
my houses smaller.

As a house it is unique,
ten feet by ten,
the height no more than seven.

With no commitment
to any one place
I laid no claim to the land.

I laid planks
upon the ground
and covered it simply.
The joints are held
with metal hasps.

This is so
I can quickly move
if something should displease me.

No trouble to rebuild,
for it would fill just two carts,
the only cost
the carter's fee.

I hide myself away
deep in the hills of Hino.*

On the east side
I have added a three-foot awning
and use the space below
to strip and burn brushwood.

By the south wall
I laid down a bamboo mat
and west of that
a shelf for offertory goods.

On the north side
behind a screen
        an image of Amida
and next to it, Fugen.
In front of them
        the Lotus Sutra.*

On the eastern side
bedding of dried bracken
for night's rest.

In the southwest
    a bamboo ledge
with three black leather-lined baskets
for poetry and music,
and works like the *Ojo-yoshu*.*

Next to the shelf,
against the wall,
a koto and a biwa,
known as "folding" koto,
"jointed" biwa.*

Such is
my little home
in this world.

Outside, to the south,
    a water pipe
with stones
to hold the water.

A wood nearby
provides twigs and kindling
in abundance.

The hills are called Toyama,
and spindletrees shade the paths.

The valley is thick with trees
but I have a view
of the Western heavens,
focus for meditation.

In the spring, wisteria,
        rippling like waves,
blooming like a holy purple cloud,
also to the west.

In summer, cuckoos.
As they chatter on I ask them
to be sure to guide me
through the mountain paths
        of death.

In autumn
the voices of evening cicadas
fill the ear.

They seem to grieve
this husk of a world.

Then in winter—
        snow!
It settles
        just like human sin
and melts,
        in atonement.

When in no mood for chanting
nor caring to read sutras
I can choose to rest.

I can be lazy if I like—
no one here to hinder me,
no one in whose eyes
to feel ashamed.

I took no vow of silence,
yet perforce observe one,
as I am alone.

I need not try so hard
to obey commandments.
Little chance to break them here!

In the morning
when my heart is full of
        "the white-topped wake
        that flows astern" *
I look out at the boats
plying round Okanoya*
and write, in the manner of Manshami.

In the evening
when the wind blows
through the katsura tree
and makes its leaves dance
I think of the Jin-yo River*
and play, imitating Gentotoku.*

When the mood takes me,
again and again, I play
        the "Song of Autumn Breezes"
to the wind in the pines
        or "Flowing Water" *
to the sound of the stream.

Though little skilled
I do not play
to please another's ear.

I play just for myself
and sing to give sustenance to my own heart.

There is a simple hut
of brushwood
at the foot of the hill
where the mountainkeeper lives.

And there is a little boy
who sometimes visits.

When all is still
I walk with this companion.
He is ten, I am sixty,
so the difference is great.

Yet both delight.
We pick buds and shrubs
and gather bulbs and herbs.*
Or go to the fields
at the foot of the hill
and gather fallen ears of rice
and make different shapes.

When the day is fine
we climb to the hilltops
and look at the sky
above my former home.

We can see Kowata hills,*
Fushimi, Toba, and Hatsukashi.

A place of beauty
has no owner.
So there is nothing
to spoil the pleasure.

When we are fit
and feel like going farther
we walk the hills
through Sumiyama,
beyond Kasatori,
visit Iwama,
or make pilgrimage to Ishiyama.

Or we make our way across
the fields of Awazu
and visit the former home
of the poet Semimaru,*
or cross Tagami River
to the grave of Sarumaro.*

Coming back,
depending on the season,
we look at cherry blossoms,
view maples, pluck bracken,
gather nuts as offerings
or to take home.

On quiet nights
I recall friends
    while looking at the moon
    through the window.

I listen to
the distant cries of monkeys
and tears wet my sleeves.

Fireflies in the bushes
then appear like fishermen's braziers
off on Makinoshima.*

The morning rain
feels like a storm
beating on the leaves.

When I hear
the tuneful cries
of copper pheasants
they sound just like
my father and mother.

When deer from higher up
come tamely down to me
I realize how far I am
from the world.

Awakening at night and
poking embers from the ashes
this old man finds his company.

The mountains do not daunt me,*
so I enjoy the hooting of the owl.
Each passing season
brings its own enchantment.

Of course, a more perceptive man
would find much more
to charm.

When I moved here
I did not mean to stay this long,
but five years have now passed.

This rough shelter
has become my home.

Rotting leaves pile up on the roof.
Moss grows on the lower parts.

Occasional word of the capital
tells me many lords have
passed away while I was hidden
here in the hills.
Others too, of lesser rank,
—numbers we can never know.

I wonder how many houses
burned down in the constant fires.

But nothing happens here
in my little hut.

Small as it is
there is room to sleep at night
and sit by day.

Space enough
for one man.

The hermit crab prefers a tiny shell
aware of its needs.

Ospreys live by the rocky coast
fearing the world of man.

And so with me.
I know my needs
and know the world.

I wish for nothing
and do not work
to acquire things.

Quiet is my only wish,
to be free from worry
happiness enough.

People in the world
do not build houses
to suit their real needs.

They build houses
for wives, children, retinues.
Or they build for friends
and those around them.

Some build houses
for masters and teachers.
And even for their treasures,
        oxen, horses.

I have built for myself,
            alone.

You may wonder why.

        The world today has its ways
        and I have mine.

I have no companion here
and no attendant either.
Even if I built bigger
who would I receive here,
who would I have to live in it?

        In their friends
people like to see a certain affluence
and the ready smile.

They seldom care for
warmth and truthfulness.

So why not find your friends
in song and nature?

Servants value tangible rewards
as well as constant favors.
They seek no care or sympathy
nor contentedness or harmony.

Why not be your own servant?
But how to be a servant?

When there is something to be done,
    employ your body.

It is hard, yet simpler
than using someone else,
and being obliged.

When you need to go somewhere
    use your feet.

This too is hard, but not as hard
as worrying about horse and saddle,
    ox and cart.

Now, I divide my body
and I give it twofold purpose.
My hands are my servants,
my legs my carriage.

This suits me well.

My heart knows
my strength's limit,
and makes me rest when I am tired.
I work again when ready.

I exert myself,
but never to excess.
So even when fatigued,
I'm not distressed.

Always walking,
always working
makes the spirit strong.

Why rest without need?

Using others is a sin.
Why should I wish
to use another?

Just the same
with food and clothing.

My clothes are arrowroot,
my bedding hemp.
I make do with what I find
     for dress.

Starwort from the fields,
berries from the hills
are all I need of sustenance.

Not mingling with society
my appearance does not matter.
My food being meager
tastes all the sweeter.

     I do not speak
of these pleasures
to reproach the rich.

I just compare
my past life
with the present.

Reality depends
upon your mind alone.*

If your mind is not at peace
what use are riches?
The grandest hall
will never satisfy.

I love my lonely dwelling,
                this one-room hut.

Sometimes I go to the capital
and am aware
I look like a begging monk.

But when I return
I pity those who seek
the dross of the world.

If you doubt my words,
consider the fish and birds.

Fish do not hate the water.
But then, none can know*
the happiness of the fish
unless he is one.

Birds love the woods.
If you are not a bird
you will not know its truths.

A quiet life is much the same.
How would anyone know it
without living it?

        The moon
of my life is setting.
The life now left me
sinks into the hills.

Any time now
I may descend
to the darkness
of the river below.

                To what end
                do I pour this out?

Buddha taught
we must not be
attached.

Yet the way I love this hut
is itself attachment.

To be attached
to the quiet and serene
must likewise be a burden.

No more time shall I waste
speaking of useless pleasures.

❀ ❀ ❀

*T*he morning is quiet
and I have meditated much
on the holy teaching.

This is what I ask myself—

*You left the world
to live in the woods,
to quiet your mind
and live the Holy Way.*

*But though you appear
to be a monk
your heart is soaked in sin.*

*Your home is modeled on
that of Vimalakirti.
Your practices are not as mindful
as those of Suddhipanthaka.**

*Is your lowly life
—surely a consequence of past deeds—
troubling you now?*

Has your discerning mind
just served to drive you mad?

To these questions of mind,
there is no answer.
    So now
I use my impure tongue
to offer a few prayers
to Amida and then
          silence.

❀ ❀ ❀

Written by
the monk Ren-in*
in a hut in Toyama,
about the last day
of the third month
of the second year
of Kenryaku

Notes

The existence of various editions of *Hojoki* in Japanese has led to a number of misinterpretations and mistranslations. The oldest and most reliable edition is the so-called *Daifukukoji* version, a handwritten copy dating to the early Kamakura Period (1192–1333), sometimes wrongly supposed to have been rendered by Chomei himself. This edition, now in the Kyoto National Museum, is the basis of most modern editions and of the present translation. Other popularized or shortened versions vary in their descriptions of Chomei's hut. They also lack at least parts of the early "disasters" and include poetry by another hand.

page 34: the third year of Angen
The year 1177, in the reign of Emperor Takakura. On

August 4 of that year the era name changed to Jisho. The fourth month was actually early summer; the twenty-eighth day would be the night before new moon.

page 34: Higuchi-Tominokoji

Higuchi was a street that ran east-west, south of Gojo. Tominokoji was a street that ran north-south, just west of Higashi-Kyogoku Street. Almost all the place names recorded in *Hojoki* exist today, although occasionally the locations have moved somewhat. The palace was to the west of the present-day palace, called the *Gosho*, in the north-central part of the city.

page 38: the fourth year of Jisho

The year 1180, in the reign of Emperor Antoku. The whirlwind struck Kyoto in the spring. In June of that year, the capital was moved west to Fukuhara, the western part of present-day Kobe City. In November it was moved back to Kyoto. This was a year of great social turbulence. The move of the capital is believed to have been the idea of Taira-no-Kiyomori, Chief Minister (*Dajo-daijin*), whose clan was to be subsequently defeated in 1185 in the Heike Civil War. Yoritomo, of the victorious Minamoto clan, inaugurated the Kamakura shogunate in the east in July 1192.

page 38: Nakamikudo-Kyogoku

The intersection of Nakamikado and Kyogoku avenues. From Nakamikado to Rokujo was about 2 kilometers.

page 40: in the reign of Saga

Saga, the fifty-second emperor, reigned from 809 to 823. Heian-kyo (the name for Kyoto at this time) was actually founded in 794, in the reign of Emperor Kanmu, so Chomei was clearly mistaken about the foundation of the city. However, there is a theory that Kyoto may not in fact have become the official capital until the time of Saga.

page 41: Yodo River

It has its source in Lake Biwa, west of Kyoto. From Kyoto it flows southwest to Osaka bay. The Yodo was an important waterway for shipping passengers and cargo.

page 44: certain wise rulers

Chomei is referring to familiar episodes relating to different two rulers, the first a legendary Chinese emperor, Yao, and the other the Japanese emperor Nintoku, possibly also legendary. The story concerning the former appears in the Chinese history *Shih Chi*; that concerning the latter in the chronicles *Nihonshoki* and *Kojiki*.

page 45: the Yowa era
The famine took place in 1181–82, in the reign of Emperor Antoku.

page 49: Ryugyo-hoin . . . Ninna-ji . . . the holy mark
Ryugyo was a son of Minamoto-no-Toshitaka. *Hoin* was the highest rank of Buddhist monks accorded by the court. Ninna-ji was—and is—a major temple of the Shingon sect located in Ukyo-ku, Kyoto, founded by the Cloistered Emperor Uda. The holy mark of the last rites was *aji*, the first letter of the Old Sanskrit alphabet. Said to be the source of all sounds and alphabets, in Shingon this character was used as a symbol of the elimination of earthly desires, and placing it on the forehead meant sending the dead to an afterlife beyond bondage to this world (*jobutsu*).

page 50: Ichijo and Kujo. . . Kyogoku and Suzaku
The area described was the Sakyo area, the eastern side of the capital, the principal part of the city at that time.

page 50: Shirakawa, Nishi-no-kyo

Shirakawa is a river that runs into the Kamo River, but here it refers to the area to the east, between the Kamo River and Higashiyama. Nishi-no-kyo was the western half of the capital, at that time not developed.

page 50: the years of Chosho

The years 1132–35.

page 51: when was it?

It was actually in the second year of Genryaku (1185).

page 53: four elements

In Buddhism earth, water, fire, and wind were believed to be the four elements which made up the universe.

page 53: the years of Saiko

The years 854–57.

page 59: I came into property

Chomei had probably been adopted by his father's mother. He inherited her house and property.

page 59: came death, my family split . . .

This literally means the relation was severed; this is

usually understood to refer to the death of Chomei's father and Chomei's relationship to the grandmother's family becoming more distant.

page 60: Mount Ohara

This is almost certainly the present-day Ohara to the northeast of Kyoto, as Chomei had befriended a monk there, although there was no mountain called Mount Ohara. So-called Ohara-yama is actually southwest of Kyoto.

page 62: the hills of Hino

Hino is in the southeastern part of present-day Kyoto City, in Fushimi Ward. It is known now for the temple Hokai-ji. The hills are behind this temple. These hills were also known as Toyama.

page 62: the Lotus Sutra

Amida is the Japanese name for the Tathagata Amita-bha, associated with the popular belief that chanting his name leads one to be received in the Western Paradise. The Pure Land faith holds that Amida takes the newly dead to Paradise borne on a purple cloud. Fugen is the Japanese name for Samantabhadra, one of the bodhisattvas often depicted with Shakamuni guarding him at his side, the other being Monju (Manjushiri), the bodhisattva of wisdom and intellect. Fugen is the bodhisattva of intellect and compassion, often invoked in prayers for longevity. Usually depicted riding a white elephant. The Lotus Sutra (*Hoke-kyo*) is one of the most important sutras in Mahayana Buddhism.

page 63: Ojo-yoshu

A devotional collection of scriptural excerpts, mainly concerning the Western Paradise, taken from various older sources. This is a most important volume as it influenced the flowering of faith in the Pure Land.

page 63: folding koto . . . jointed biwa

A "folding koto" could literally be folded in half, while a "jointed" biwa had a detachable neck, for ease of carrying.

page 65: "the white-topped wake that flows astern"

The line refers to a poem by Manzei-shami (sometimes, as here, abbreviated to Manshami) in the eighth-century anthology *Man'yoshu*: "What shall I liken this world to? / It is like all traces of the white-topped waves / left by the morning boats / and now quite gone."

page 65: Okanoya

A town by the river in present-day Uji City. To the southwest of Hino.

page 65: the Jin-yo River

The Xunyang, that flows into the Yangtze. This is a reference to a poem by Pai Lo-tien: "I saw off a guest one night / at the side of the Xunyang / Maple leaves and flowers of reeds / in the lonely autumn."

page 65: Gentotoku

A high-ranking eleventh-century court officer who was a poet and master biwa player. His style of music was known as Katsura style.

page 65: "Autumn Breezes" . . . "Flowing Water"

"Song of Autumn Breezes" ("Shufuraku") is a piece of music written for koto. It is thought to be the music of Amida coming to take one to Paradise. "Flowing Water" ("Ryusen") is for biwa and is music reserved for the initiated.

page 66: . . . bulbs and herbs

The plants listed in this section in the original are cogon grass (*mebana*); "rock-pear" (*iwanashi*), a shrub in the rhododendron family that bears small white round-shaped fruit in spring; bulbil (*nukago*), also very small and round, which grows from the joints of the leaves of yam; and dropwort (*seri*).

page 66: *Kowata hills* . . .

All the places mentioned here and following are *uta-makura*, places famed in poetry. They can be seen from the top of the hill behind Hino, toward the west and in order from the nearest to the farthest. Sumiyama and Kasatori are to the east of Hino. Iwama and Ishiyama both refer to temples, Iwama-dera and Ishiyama-dera in present-day Otsu City. Awazu is the present-day Awazu-cho, in Otsu City. This was formerly the site of a pine forest by Lake Biwa.

page 67: *Semimaru*

In the original, Semiuta-no-okina refers to the poet Semimaru. Semiuta was a kind of song played on a koto. The term probably meant an old man who was a master performer of semiuta. The place referred to is probably the shrine Seki-no-myojin, dedicated to Semimaru.

page 67: Sarumaro

In the original, Sarumaro Mochigimi, the latter word probably referring to his court rank. He is thought to have been a poet, although nothing definite is known about him.

page 68: Makinoshima

In present-day Uji City.

page 68: The mountains do not daunt me

This is a reference to a poem by Saigyo (1118–90): "Deep in the mountains / No sounds of birds around me / Only the frightful sounds of owls." In fact, Chomei wishes us to understand a contrary feeling, that unlike the great Saigyo he has no awe for the hills: the truth is he may not even be so deep in them.

page 75: Reality depends . . .

The term used is the Buddhist one, *sangai*, literally, "the three worlds": the world of desire, the world of "color" and the world without "color." The world of desire is the lowest and is for those bound by sexual desire and desire for food. The world of "color" is for those who are rid of these two desires. The things in this world are all very fine and delicate. The world without "color" is the highest and is for beings who are rid of all earthly desires. It is for those in constant meditation.

page 75: none can know . . .
The phrase was borrowed from Chuang Tzu.

page 77: Vimalakirti . . . Suddhipanthaka
Vimalakirti (Jomyokoji in the original) was an enlightened disciple of Buddha who lived in a small room. There is a sutra with his name. Suddhipanthaka (Shurihandoku), also a disciple of Buddha, famously took four months to remember one short prayer but finally became *arakan* (arhat).

page 78: Ren-in
Chomei's given name as a monk. The second year of Kenryaku was 1212, in the reign of Emperor Juntoku.

YASUHIKO MORIGUCHI and DAVID JENKINS are teachers and translators who live in Kyoto. Yasuhiko Moriguchi was born in Yoshino, Nara, and was educated in Japan and the United States, where he received a bachelor's degree in philosophy. David Jenkins grew up in England and worked for several years as a journalist and editor in London and the United States. Moriguchi and Jenkins have collaborated on two previous translations of classical Japanese verse, *The Song in the Dream of the Hermit: Selections from the Kanginshu* and *The Dance of the Dust on the Rafters: Selections from Ryojin-hisho.*

MICHAEL HOFMANN is an American artist who has lived in Kyoto since 1972 studying under the painter/priest Jikihara Gyokusei.

OTHER TITLES FROM STONE BRIDGE PRESS
IN THE ROCK SPRING COLLECTION
OF JAPANESE LITERATURE

Death March on Mount Hakkoda by Jiro Nitta

Wind and Stone by Masaaki Tachihara

Still Life and Other Stories by Junzo Shono

Right under the big sky, I don't wear a hat
by Hosai Ozaki

The Name of the Flower by Kuniko Mukoda

CONTEMPORARY JAPANESE WOMEN'S POETRY
A Long Rainy Season: Haiku and Tanka
Other Side River: Free Verse
edited by Leza Lowitz, Miyuki Aoyama,
and Akemi Tomioka

Basho's Narrow Road: Spring and Autumn Passages
by Matsuo Basho, with commentary by Hiroaki Sato

Naked by Shuntaro Tanikawa

Milky Way Railroad by Kenji Miyazawa